LATCHMERE PUB

T0262431

The Most Humane Way to Kill a Lobster

By **Duncan Macmillan**

First performed at Theatre 503 at the Latchmere Pub on 1 March 2005

Theatre 503 presents

THE MOST HUMANE WAY
TO KILL A LOBSTER
by **Duncan Macmillan**

Loretta Spencer	Holly de Jong
Sophie Spencer	Jenny Maddox
Policewoman	Rosie Thomson
Pregnant Woman	Laura Sanchez
Barnaby Castle	Martin Johnston
Victims Support Group Members	Members of the company
Understudy	Hayley Doherty

Director	Clare Lizzimore
Designer	Paul Burgess
Sound Designer	Theo Holloway
Lighting Designer	Phil Hewitt
Stage Manager	Gemma Garner
Costume Assistant	Julie Landau

Theatre 503 at the Latchmere Pub
503 Battersea Park Road
London SW11 3BW
Admin / Fax: 020 7978 7041
Box Office: 020 7978 7040
www.theatre503.com
email: info@theatre503.com

Writer

Duncan Macmillan

Duncan Macmillan studied Playwriting at Birmingham University and Central School of Speech and Drama, and Film and Theatre at Reading University. He has also been a member of the Soho Theatre Young Writers Group. This is his first play, written whilst on attachment to the Royal Court Theatre Young Writers Programme, where he is currently a member of the Invitation Group. His play *From Here to the Moon* was chosen alongside *The Most Humane Way to Kill a Lobster* by the Royal Court as the Play of the Season, and presented as a rehearsed reading in January 2005.

Cast

Holly de Jong Loretta Spencer

Holly's theatre work includes, in the West End: *The Master Builder*, *Phèdre* (also in New York for the Almeida Theatre) and *Godspell*. For the National Theatre: *A Month in the County*, *Don Juan* and *In Boxes*. Other Theatre includes: *The White Crow (Eichmann in Jerusalem)* at the Mercury Studio; *Villette* (Sheffield Crucible); *Relative Values*, *After you with the Milk*, *Wild Things* (Salisbury Playhouse); *Billy Liar*, *Stags and Hens* (Newcastle Playhouse); *And a Nightingale Sang* (Oxford Playhouse); *Blithe Spirit* (Everyman Cheltenham). Holly's television work has included: *The Duchess of Duke Street*, *Penmarric*, *Lytton's Diary*, *Van der Valk*, *Poirot*, *Matilda's England*, *The Weather in the Streets*, *Goodbye and I Hope we Meet Again*, *Love for Lydia*, *Casualty*, *Brushstokes*, *The Detectives*, *The File on Jill Hatch*, *Titmus Regained*, *The Assassination Run*, *Eastenders*, *The Chief*, *Doctors*, *Daniel Deronda*, and Lady Farrow in *Blackadder II*. Films have included: *Aliens* (Newt's mother), *Electric Dreams*, *Everyone's Happy*, *The Hiding Place* and *Soaked*. Radio and Audio work has included: *Definitely The Bahamas*, *Bedrock*, *Letters From a Second Home in Picardy*, *What Happened With Saint George*, *Dr Who*, *Tales from the Decameron* and *550 Degrees North*.

Jenny Maddox Sophie Spencer

Jenny studied Film and Drama at the University of Reading before training in performance at Central School of Speech and Drama. Recent theatre credits include: *Killer Joe* (Bristol Old Vic), *Educating Rita* (Brewhouse Theatre, Taunton), *Pool Party* (Alma Theatre, Bristol), *Doomed Youth* (National Tour), *Time Tunnel* (National Tour), *The Window Cleaner* (Chelsea Theatre), *Girls* (Southwark Playhouse), *How To Teach A Fish To Walk* (Battersea Arts Centre).

Rosie Thomson Policewoman / Member of Victims Support Group

Rosie trained at the Drama Centre, London. Her theatre credits include: *Henna Night* (Chelsea Theatre), directed by Caroline Hadley. Work in television includes: *The Bill*, *Second Sight*, *Family Affairs*, *Judge John Deed*, *A Touch of Frost*, *Dream Team* and *Eastenders*. Film work includes: *Enigma* (directed by Michael Apted).

Laura Sanchez Pregnant Woman / Member of Victims Support Group

Laura graduated from The Bristol Old Vic Theatre School in July 2004. Her theatre credits include: Morgan le Fay in *Merlin and The Winter King* (Derby Playhouse), Angel in *Paradise Lost* (Bristol Old Vic) and Adele in *Les Liaisons Dangereuses* (Bristol Old Vic).

Martin Johnston Barnaby Castle

Most recent theatre includes: President Roosevelt and Bert Healy in *Annie – The Musical* (Aberystwyth Arts Centre); Dr Conrad Fuller in the British musical premiere of *On A Clear Day You Can See Forever* (Bridewell Theatre); *Dr Jekyll and Mr Hyde* (Major Road Theatre Company tour); and Herbert Parchester in the UK tour of *Me and My Girl*. Opera includes: several seasons with the Royal Opera Company at Covent Garden including productions of *Turandot*, *Boris Godunof*, *Tosca*, *Rigoletto* and *Peter Grimes* (also at La Scala Opera House, Milan). He has worked extensively in drama, theatre-in-education and community theatre with companies such as Leicestershire Schools Theatre Company; Roundabout Theatre Company, Nottingham; Action Transport Theatre, Cheshire; and Theatre Van, Harlow.

Hayley Doherty Understudy

Hayley trained at Bristol Old Vic Theatre School, graduating in 2004. Theatre credits include: David Farr's *Paradise Lost* for the Bristol Old Vic Company and *Raising Zygmunt* (New Plays North West) directed by Stefan Escreet. Television credits include: Dee Briscoe in *The Bill* (Thames TV) and Jennifer in *Silent Witness* (BBC1). Short Film: Kate in *Ladies* (Ignition Films). Whilst in training theatre credits included: Juliet in *Romeo and Juliet*, Jailer's Daughter in *The Two Noble Kinsmen*, Rowena in *Salad Days*, Annie Marten in *The Murder in the Red Barn*, Lady Bountiful/Gypsy in *The Beaux' Stratagem* and Audrey in *Blue Remembered Hills* (for radio).

Company

Clare Lizzimore Director

Clare trained as a director at Central School of Speech and Drama. In 2002 she set up Sphinx Theatre Company's Writers Group, with resident writer Amy Rosenthal, where she produced and directed three new writing festivals including over fourteen new plays and readings at Southwark Playhouse, Chelsea Theatre and Greenwich Theatre. She also directed *Find Me Here* (a short piece devised for *The Young Vic: Shorts,* in response to Gísli Örn Garðarsson's *Romeo and Juliet*). As an assistant director she has worked on the 24hour plays at The Old Vic, on Kwame Kwei-Armah's short *Final Call*, assisted Vicky Featherstone on Jennifer Farmer's *180°c* (Paines Plough Wild Lunch Season '05 at The Young Vic) and supported Simon Stephens on the Royal Court Young Writers Programme, where she will direct the Play of the Season. She also works in drama development at the BBC, has been short-listed for the JMK director's award 2005, and will be part of this year's National Theatre Directors Programme. This is Clare's debut directing a full-length play.

Paul Burgess Designer

Paul trained at Motley Theatre Design Course, following a degree in English at Oxford. Recent designs include sets for *Much Ado About Nothing* (Shakespeare's Globe) and *The People's Opera* (touring), sets and video for *Choked* (touring) and *The Three Vs* (touring) and sets and costumes for *Cancer Time* (Theatre 503), *Flush* (Soho Theatre), *Party Time/One for the Road* (Battersea Arts Centre). *Peer Gynt* (Arcola Theatre), *Have I None* (Southwark Playhouse) *Sherlock Holmes and the Secret of Making Whoopee* (La Tea, NYC), *Women and Criminals* (Here Arts Centre, NYC) and *Fred and Madge* (Oxford Playhouse). Assistant designing includes *The Ramayana* (National Theatre), *Twelfth Night* (Shakespeare's Globe, US tour) and work for Tara Arts. Film includes co-designing/advising on five films for Ghanaian TV. Directing credits include creating a new work, *Out of Nothing*, for The Junction, Cambridge, and *Selfish*, a commission for The Arches, Glasgow. He also designed set and video for both projects. He co-founded the experimental arts company Scale Project, which has created work in the UK and Siberia and was part of the gold award-winning British Display at the 2003 Prague Quadrennial. He also works for the creative and performing arts charity Youth CREATE.

Theo Holloway Sound Designer

Theo's sound design credits include: *Norfolk's Rose* (Wilde Theatre, Bracknell), *Miss Julie* (King's Cross Courtyard), *The Age of Consent* (The Bush Theatre), and several commissions for Sphinx Theatre Company's Writers Group. He wrote the musical *The Damnation Game* for South Hill Park's Festival of New Writing, toured as a sound engineer with Matthew Bourne's *Nutcracker*, and is currently Senior Sound Technician for the RSC's Spanish Golden Age season at the Playhouse.

Phil Hewitt Lighting Designer

Phil trained at Theatr Clwyd, and at LAMDA, graduating in 1992. Recent lighting designs include: *God is a DJ*, *Talkin' Loud*, *Ministry of Pleasure*, and *Fishbowl* at Theatre 503; *Nymphs and Shepherds* at the Etcetera; *Talk* for Sweetspot TC, Brighton; *Manband* for Brian at Battersea Arts Centre; *Debris* for Theatre 503 in Battersea, Germany and Edinburgh; *Migrant Overtures* for Sleeping Dogs in Battersea and Brighton; *Mortal Ladies Possessed* for Linda Marlowe at the Mill, Guildford and tour. He is also a sound designer, having been Head of Sound at the Thorndike Theatre, Leatherhead, where he launched a number of national tours and West End shows with various companies, including the Peter Hall Company. He is currently Technical Co-ordinator of *Live '05* at Chelsea Theatre; a part of the theatre collective Brian, whose *Billie Holliday* will be running for three weeks in Battersea Arts Centre in April; a composer of electronic music; and an Associate Director of Theatre 503.

Gemma Garner Stage Manager

Since graduating from Central School of Speech and Drama in 2004, Gemma has worked at the 2004 Edinburgh Fringe Festival with *Dude! Where's my Teddy Bear?* and *Waitin' for Da G!* (Modify the Van) as well as *The Bottle* (Conspirators' Kitchen) and a tour to Warsaw with *Romeo and Juliet – The Panto!* (CTheatre). Other work outside Central includes: *The Ministry of Pleasure* (Theatre 503), *Debris* (Battersea Arts Centre), *Orientations* (Border Crossings Theatre Co), *Verdi's Il Trittico* (Hampstead Garden Opera). Central productions include: *Absolute Hell*, *The Odyssey* (The Minack Theatre, Cornwall), *Plasticine*, *Dancing at Lughnasa* and *Richard the Second*. Gemma has also worked briefly as a runner for *Family Affairs* (Talkback Thames).

Julie Landau Costume Assistant

Julie graduated from Central School of Speech and Drama with an MA in Scenography. She has since worked as a scenographer on a number of productions including: *Fear and Loathing on the Kings Road* (Chelsea Theatre) and *Sphinx Shorts* (Greenwich Theatre) both for Sphinx Theatre, *Waiting for the Parade* and *Elegies for Angels, Punks and Raging Queens*, both for Mountview, *Photostory* (Komedia, Edinburgh and Battersea Arts Centre), *Invertigo* (Broadway Theatre) and *Handy Pantomime* (Pleasance).

THEATRE 503 AT THE LATCHMERE PUB

Theatre 503 recently won The Empty Space Peter Brook Award 2004, and is one of London's most exciting studio theatres. Since September 2002 we have been dedicated to new writing: staging new plays and discovering important new playwrights.

'A night here offers a chance to experience the new, the exciting and the raw before anyone else.' Guardian

Since 2002, Theatre 503 has staged plays by Dennis Kelly, Phil Porter, Ursula Rani Sarma, Jennifer Farmer, Ronan O'Donnell, Samantha Ellis, Glyn Cannon, Peter Morris, Trevor Williams, Said Sayrafiezadeh, Falk Richter, Anna Marie Murphy as well as new plays by more established playwrights such as Ron Hutchinson, Naomi Wallace and Fraser Grace.

'Consistently unearthing some of London theatre's most exciting new voices.' Time Out

Artistic Director	Paul Higgins
Associate Directors	Phil Hewitt
	Johnnie Lyne-Pirkis
Artistic Associate	Jenny MacDonald
Literary Associate	Matt Morrison
Theatre Administrator	Anna Bewick

Friends of Theatre 503:
Colin Clarke, Sir Ian Holm, Kenneth Branagh, Ness Valley Films, Peter Heslop, Haig Tahta, TandT Properties, Rikki Tahta, Graham Moody, David Tringham, Mardy Griffin, Patrick Whitter, Georgina Winbourne, Marianne Badrichani, Barbara Naughton, Matt Lewis, Vicki Fraser, George Chisholm.

We would like to thank the following for their continued support: Richard Lee and the rest of the team at the Jerwood Space, Michael Rodgers and Chris Mullin at Barracuda Group Ltd, Andrew Higgins.

Plays premiered at Theatre 503 and published by Oberon Books include:
Touched... / Blue by Ursula Rani Sarma, *Stealing Sweets and Punching People* by Phil Porter, *Debris* by Dennis Kelly, *Ministry of Pleasure* by Craig Baxter and *One Glass Wall* by Danusia Iwaszko.

All Oberon titles are available from **www.oberonbooks.com**.

Duncan Macmillan

THE MOST HUMANE WAY TO KILL A LOBSTER

OBERON BOOKS
LONDON

WWW.OBERONBOOKS.COM

First published in 2005 by Oberon Books Ltd
521 Caledonian Road, London N7 9RH
Tel: +44 (0) 20 7607 3637 / Fax: +44 (0) 20 7607 3629
e-mail: info@oberon.books.com
www.oberonbooks.com

Reprinted in 2011, 2015

A catalogue record for this book is available from the British
Library.

PB ISBN: 978-1-84002-559-0
E ISBN: 978-1-84943-720-2

Cover image: www.photonica.com

Visit www.oberonbooks.com to read more about all our books
and to buy them. You will also find features, author interviews and
news of any author events, and you can sign up for e-newsletters
so that you're always first to hear about our new releases.

Characters

LORETTA SPENCER, fifty

SOPHIE SPENCER, thirteen, Loretta's daughter

POLICEWOMAN, late thirties

VICTIMS SUPPORT GROUP MEMBERS

PREGNANT WOMAN, twenty

BARNABY CASTLE, fifty-eight

Author's note: A space between lines of dialogue indicates a pause. The longer the space, the longer the pause.

The author wishes to thank
Simon Stephens and Nina Lyndon at the Royal Court,
and Will Hammond.

1

A police station. Pale blue walls. A small window. A white wall clock. A water dispenser. A table. Two clear plastic cups. Four grey plastic chairs around the table, another next to a waste paper bin by the door. A pin-board covered in school photos of young girls, two black and white Ordnance Survey maps covered in yellow and pink pen marks, and several Post-it notes.

LORETTA is surrounded by shopping bags and sits opposite a uniformed POLICEWOMAN who is making notes on a piece of paper.

Outside it is snowing.

LORETTA   The idea is to cause as little suffering as possible. I'm going to kill it. I'm going to eat it. But I don't want to torture it.

Do you understand?

So you put it in the freezer. Alive. It slowly loses consciousness, so when you transfer it to the boiling water it doesn't feel a thing. It's asleep, you see? The boiling water kills the lobster fairly instantaneously which

I'm not sure how they know this. I'm not sure how they know what the lobster feels in its final moments. With its lobster memories flashing in front of its antennae.

What am I saying?

I suppose that

13

this is how I've felt.
Recently.

That I've been asleep. I've been in some deep freeze and suddenly I can feel steam in my face, falling headlong into scalding

no.
That's not what I'm
that's not
that's not what I'm trying to say at all.

At all.

What I said before

I never said it was, that this man, I don't even know if I should give his name because it really wasn't as if

I mean, I never thought, not for a minute, that not at the time anyway, that

I'm sorry.

LORETTA drinks some water.

I have a daughter.
Do you have children?

I think there's been a mistake, you see. I think you're seeing me because the girl at the front, she thought I said

I was confused. I'd been shopping and I'd started to cry and before I knew it I was in here.

I've been following the case, the missing girl. Little Eleanor Lucas. The woman at the front, I think she thought I had information about that, which is why I'm here with you now. Is that what she
well, anyway. I wish I did. I don't. Not about
that.

The POLICEWOMAN clicks her pen and places it back on her pad.

I'm sorry, I'm really gabbling. I can hear myself talking and I'm really, you know, gabbling. I'm actually not much of a talker.
At all.
It's just
these places I find very intimidating.
I have a thing about chairs. Certain chairs
make me
anyway. Not relevant. But it's to do with the plastic chairs I think.

The girls, the man that has been arrested, the papers said there were girls, more each day, who have come forward and said that they were, that they have had, you know, in the past that they have been
that they
I was reading about this and, I think I'm right in saying that the eldest was twenty-seven and the youngest was twelve.
Some of them tried to prosecute but it never got anywhere. I think that's right.

Anyway, one fourteen year-old said that he wasn't aggressive, I know he was with some of them, I know that with at least one of them he used that

you know.

But with this girl, he'd been with her, seeing her, for a few weeks and they'd slept together and she then reported him, or at least she tried to, for

for what? For child abuse.

Anyway, it got me thinking. How did she know?

She was fourteen. This is how she lost her virginity. To an older man who paid her attention, who had a car, who let her smoke cigarettes and drink vodka and Red Bull in his house.

How did she know it was child abuse? If it wasn't, if *he* wasn't

I'm sorry, I'm kind of still thinking this through, you know, out loud, because something is occurring to me and it hasn't quite

surfaced yet. So I appreciate you listening. I know that's your job, but still. I know you're allowing me to talk, hoping I'll reveal something crucial, but I assure you I don't know anything.

Honestly.

I know you've got more important things. So thanks.

The POLICEWOMAN looks at the wall clock, closes her notepad and sits back.

At fourteen, I'm sure I had no conception of myself as being a child. I knew I was young, but a *child*?

16

I lost my virginity at fourteen. I slept with a man named Barnaby Castle. He was twenty-two.

I've never told anybody this until now.

The POLICEWOMAN opens a drawer in the table and takes a single tissue which she offers to LORETTA.

Thank you.
I really am sorry.

The POLICEWOMAN opens her pad, clicks her pen and writes something down.

If you're writing down 'Barnaby Castle', you really don't have to. I know you have to, of course you do. But you really don't. I don't intend to press charges. It's hard enough prosecuting someone for rape, let alone something that happened thirty years ago.

The POLICEWOMAN continues to write. LORETTA watches her.

If you're writing down 'rape', it was just a figure of speech. I've never been raped. Nobody has ever forced me to

not ever. I know you have to write that down, but seriously.

I know what a grave thing it is to make a statement. I take that very seriously.

I suppose what I've been thinking is that those girls and women who spoke to the police, I know that it didn't stop him, but I just thought how brave. How brave, particularly the littler ones, to go to the police and talk about something so

to relive the experience. All that to try to help, to try to make sure that it can't happen again, that this man could never

I mean, I know it didn't work. And he went on to kill at least that one little girl.

But still. How brave.

I know that when I was fourteen I couldn't have done that.

I wouldn't have known.

I wouldn't have understood that there was anything

I didn't

LORETTA suddenly laughs and puts her head in her hands.

I am so sorry. What am I doing? I've been under a lot of pressure. My daughter is getting to that age and my job is

you know.

Don't pay any attention to me.

Please. Throw your notes in the bin and forget I wasted so much of

I'm so sorry.

LORETTA begins to cry quietly. The POLICEWOMAN reopens the drawer, this time taking out the entire box of tissues. LORETTA sees the box and smiles.

I'm hopeless. Thank you.

She blows her nose.

Stupid.
Stupid stupid stupid.

What a selfish stupid bitch.
Sorry.

I'm thinking about something that happened thirty years ago. There's photos of that poor girl's teeth under that paving slab, those forensic teams wearing white suits and masks carrying bin bags in the woods, somewhere that desperate family sleepless and sick and here I am taking up time, here I am thinking about
      me.

And I'm fine. Whatever I went through, and it was really nothing, but isn't it, I mean, it's about the effect it has on you, on your life, and
      and I wouldn't change my life for anything.

This isn't your job. I'm sorry. I've got nothing of interest to you. I really haven't. I just need
      I need to talk to someone. But I'm sorry, I know that's not your job. I'll see someone. Professionally. I know that's what you're going to suggest I do. I appreciate that.

But what if

what if you're a middle-aged mother who's halfway around the Disney Store when she suddenly realises she may have been the victim of sexual abuse?

I don't know why I'm here. I don't know what I'm asking.

You could look at his file. See if he even has a file.
      If anyone else has

if he made a
habit

I'd hate to think that because I never said
anything, that maybe he went on and did something.
Something serious.
More serious I mean.

Because I never realised.
At fourteen I had no idea. What I thought
was my first love, what was so exciting and special at the
time, what I smugly told myself when school or home got
difficult was me becoming a woman, was me being wanted
and valued and loved was actually a stupid child without
guidance being groomed by a predatory paedophile.

Sorry. I don't mean that. There wasn't such a
thing at the time.

I remember being told, in school, not to take
sweets from strangers. There was a cartoon with a man
offering to show a child his parrot, did you ever see that?
We were trained to deal with that specific
eventuality, although my aunt had a parakeet which
was boring and stank so I wasn't that interested. I never
remember having an idea that there were men who wanted
to
that the reason we shouldn't get in cars with
strangers was that

if a man touched my daughter I would tear
him apart. I know this isn't the kind of thing I should be
saying to a police officer but if
if he
I'd never find a torture that could satisfy me.
I'd

sorry.
Sorry sorry sorry.

Sorry.

I'm experiencing feelings of anger for some
reason.

LORETTA finishes her water. She sees the pictures of young girls on the pin-board.

There'll be another.

Won't there?

The POLICEWOMAN takes her cup, walks to the water dispenser and fills it. The POLICEWOMAN keeps her back to LORETTA during the following.

There'll be other girls. Like there have been others before, there'll be more to come. More little body parts in bin bags found in quarries and burnt out cars. More smiling school photos on the front pages. More tearful pleading press conferences. More public eulogies, more religious groups, psychics and con men swooping down like vultures to pray on the high profile desperation, more locks on the doors, more newspapers sold, more tiny changes to legislation, more

more.

The POLICEWOMAN returns to the table with the water.

Barnaby was

a friend of the family. His dad was. A friend of my father. My father wanted a boy and

Barnaby would fix the car. My father would drive him to football. Barnaby would pick me up from school sometimes.

He was
I thought he was
wonderful.
Tall.

LORETTA smiles.

He listened to me. He was the only person who

you know, who actually seemed to

most of the time I wasn't even saying anything but he was still listening. If you see what I mean. My mother has never been good at that. Even now. I don't see her much. I know I should, but

you know, she just
I just
she just sits and I talk, usually about nothing, but even so
I can see she she's not
hearing
what I'm saying.

He'd come over sometimes when my parents were out. Barnaby.

The POLICEWOMAN picks up her pen and begins to write once more.

My parents were out a lot. Work. They didn't have it easy, they

we didn't have much. At all. Not that that's
but it is though, isn't it?
This was back in Newcastle.

The POLICEWOMAN looks up at LORETTA.

I know. I've lost my accent.

Barnaby would drive me around. He'd tell me about his car. About cars in general. He'd tell me about how he was going to become a soldier. Or a musician. He had ambition. More than anyone else I knew anyway. I imagined we could run away together, get out of the town. Go somewhere better.

When it happened I'd bunked off school. We went to the aquarium. I loved it there. I felt like I was under the ocean. I'd put my face right up to the glass and feel like I could swim off. I'd stay like that for hours. Get a numb face.

He'd always play this one record, 'Who Needs Forever' by Astrud Gilberto. I think it's the only proper record he had. After we

he put on this record and I listened to it. I mean, I *really* listened to it. I thought he was trying to tell me something very specific. Personal. I loved it. I loved it I loved it.

The other day I was driving to pick up Sophie, my daughter, from a friend's, and I was listening to 'Desert Island Discs'. I can't remember who it was, but this woman, I think she's a television presenter, said that she wanted to include 'Who Needs Forever' because she listened to it with her first boyfriend.

And I suddenly felt completely robbed.

I never even considered that other people will have listened to that record. Then I thought how it might not have been personal at all, that it might be that he didn't want to talk. He was sick of listening to me. It might be this smooth thing he does every time he

like his trick. His one romantic thing. He might even have copied the idea from a friend.

There may be all these other women with that memory. Suddenly it wasn't a good, romantic, nostalgic thought. Suddenly it was frightening and lonely. They started to play it and I had to pull the car over and I just

it wasn't anger. It wasn't disgust or sadness. I don't know what emotion it was, but it hasn't quite gone away.

When I read about the killer, this man they've caught, that he'd said many of the same things to each of them, that he'd written the same things in letters, taken them to the same places

I had this horrible image of 'Who Needs Forever' being on the record player in the bedrooms of all these missing girls.

Will you check him out? Barnaby Castle? Just see.

I know it's nothing. I mentioned this to a friend of mine and she said that she lost her virginity at fourteen as well. She said that most women she knew first had sex with older men. But that's just how it was. Guys who grew up to be doctors and barristers, work

in supermarkets and schools and police stations, in the
government, in the military, on television

they can't all be child abusers.

Do you think it's still snowing?

The sound of rain.

2

LORETTA's kitchen. A counter and two tall stools. Cereal packets. A bowl of lemons. A kettle. A fridge, on which is a school photograph of SOPHIE, aged ten. It is stuck there with differently coloured magnetic letters. Also on the fridge is a large red cartoon heart.

SOPHIE is sat at the counter, resting her head in her hands and turning the pages of Heat *magazine. She looks up slowly, lost in thought.*

As she hears keys in the lock, she hides the magazine under a large chemistry textbook which she then pretends to read.

LORETTA enters, carrying her shopping. The snow has turned to rain and LORETTA is soaked.

LORETTA   Hello darling. How's school?

How did the mock exam go?

Fine Mum. Thanks for asking. Not at all. How was your day? Really terrible. Oh that's a shame, let me make you a cup of tea and you can tell me all about it. Thank you darling, you are thoughtful.

She dumps a couple of bags on the counter. SOPHIE rummages through them. LORETTA takes her coat off and hangs it up.

What is it next? Chemistry isn't it?

She lifts up the book to look at the cover.

Chemistry.

LORETTA starts the kettle boiling and produces a large pan.
SOPHIE is checking the fat content of a guacamole dip. LORETTA
takes out a chopping board.

I thought I'd make your favourite.

Hooray.

Oh well. You're good at chemistry. That
should be an easy one.

SOPHIE opens the guacamole dip and a bag of crisps and begins
to eat.

I'm not saying any of them are easy darling.
But comparatively.

Don't fill up on those.

There's always next year, anyway.
I don't know why the school is pushing you to
sit them so early.

I know I suggested it but

I'm just saying.
What have you done to your

that's a new top, what have you

is that deliberate? The rips and holes? That
top wasn't cheap.

What is it about teen angst? What happened to good pop songs? It's all misery now.

SOPHIE swings herself onto the counter where she sits against the wall.

It's big business, misery.

You're young. Enjoy life. It gets so much worse.

LORETTA pulls out a fresh lobster from one of the bags. It's alive. She puts it on the counter facing SOPHIE. SOPHIE immediately recoils her feet.
   LORETTA produces an enormous knife.

Is this about the march?

Silent treatment?

Your teachers have decided not to allow you to go and I'm not going to overrule their decision. Apart from anything, I think it's the right one.

There will be some students who will be going to London not to protest but to shop and get into trouble.

I know you're not one of those, but

anyway the war's over. It's been over for ages, I really don't see the point of going on a 'stop the war' march now.

LORETTA pours the boiling water into the pan.

I've told you, I think it's wonderful you're getting interested in politics. We'll go into the city one day and have a look at Downing Street and maybe go into the public gallery if we're allowed. I'll buy you some books on, you know, politics for beginners. How about that?

Because you've still got all that free-range chocolate the Coldplay man said to buy remember? Very expensive and not as nice as Nestlé.

And besides, your absence from the march isn't going to make any difference. Is it though?

You're young sweetheart. You've got the energy, but you don't have the knowledge or experience. Be patient. You will. Don't rush and make mistakes. Not ones you can't put right again.

You're thirteen. In years to come, you will regret almost everything you did at this age.

She takes the knife and, point first, pushes it directly down just behind the lobster's head, before cutting it in half. This gets SOPHIE's full attention.

You really want to go?

There's going to be lots and lots of people probably. It could be very dangerous.

LORETTA drops the lobster into the pan.

I didn't realise you felt so strongly about it. But I do, I do think it's great.

But you've got exams. You've got to be preparing for your own future, never mind Iraq.

SOPHIE looks up at LORETTA coldly. LORETTA wipes her hands on a tea-towel.

Is this about some boy? Someone you're trying to impress?

In disgust, SOPHIE produces headphones and begins listening to music.
    After a while, LORETTA takes some lemons from the bowl and begins to slice them.

I know you can still hear me.

I'm thinking of going away for a while. After your exams I thought we could take a trip up north to where I went to school. Newcastle. Show you all my old haunts.

Maybe catch up with some old friends. See who we can bump into.

Go and see Nan on the way up there.

Haven't seen her for a while.

And she won't be around forever.

LORETTA takes a large bowl and empties a bag of salad into it.

Go to the seaside on the way back?

Get some colour on you.

LORETTA finishes the salad and looks at SOPHIE for a while in silence. SOPHIE avoids making eye contact.

I feel like we've been missing each other. Both in the same house, sometimes both in the same room, but not really together.

When you were a baby I used to hold you in my arms and tell you stories. Just make them up. Always different. You remember?

They weren't brilliant. Not even stories, really. No beginning, middle and end. Just descriptions.

Your favourite was, do your remember, the weeping room, about the room which rained. Indoors. I don't remember how it went but you loved that story. You used to dream about it, do you remember?

Something to do with, that the room was weeping. Is that right? Crying? But it was a happy room. It was full of plants and there were all sorts of tropical fish swimming around under tables and making homes in the armchairs. Birds singing, perched on hatstands and bookshelves.

You always thought it was a real room. That it really existed somewhere. And that one day you'd see it.

I don't know when I stopped holding you and telling you stories. I just noticed that it doesn't happen anymore.

LORETTA takes the knife and chopping board to the sink. She turns quickly.

Are you ashamed of me? Do you wish you had a less middle-class background? Is that why you rip your clothes? Do you wish your mother didn't cook lobster and buy guacamole?

Do you think by being middle-class you lack something, that you have less authenticity or something?

SOPHIE turns the volume up on her headphones.

You dress nicely when we go up and see Nan.

LORETTA angrily scrubs the chopping board.

When I was growing up my mother would always make sure I was dressed nicely and that
and yes, I know I've told you this a thousand times and you're bored and ashamed of your smothering pretentious mother but when I was growing up my mum would always make sure I was,
and remember she had so little,
she would,
even though we had nothing,
she would make sure that we always

she'd be ashamed to see you vandalising perfectly good new clothes.

SOPHIE climbs off the kitchen counter and walks towards the door.

If it hadn't been for my mother we wouldn't have what we have and because of her you have been given a better start in life and you should be grateful for it you spoilt little bitch. If you want an argument then let's have one.

SOPHIE walks out, runs upstairs and slams her bedroom door.

Oh, don't, darling. Sophie. I'm sorry. It's

look, just ignore me I'm just

LORETTA sits on the stool and puts her head in her hands. After a moment, music can be heard coming through the ceiling.

LORETTA slowly moves her hands from her face and looks up at the ceiling as she recognises the song as Astrud Gilberto's 'Who Needs Forever'.

Lights fade and the quality of the sound changes to non-diagetic.

3

Seven pine straight-backed chairs arranged into a circle. Four women sit, looking at LORETTA who is standing. An electric fan.
LORETTA holds a glass filled with ice cubes.

LORETTA   Deeply romantic.
Deeply. Deeply.

My memory, what really happened, has been completely overtaken by the story I've told. The myth.
I boasted at school. I didn't tell many people really, but you know

everything. The way I walked. It was boasting.

When I try to think about it objectively I feel very

I never felt lust. I know that because I've felt it frequently since.
But I think I knew that at the time.
It wasn't about me. It was all him. I knew it's what he wanted and I wanted to

and everything about it. I have a vague memory of the pictures on his walls and his bed sheets. He had a stack of comic books. Big hard-backed books about cars. His room was quite damp. The wallpaper was peeling a little by the window. That textured paper you don't really see anymore. Painted over, you know. Eggshell yellow. His smell. The smell of his hair. His weight.

Because he was quite a bit older I thought he was so mature. In hindsight of course I know that he was quite the opposite. For his age.

Because you've got to have something a bit wrong haven't you? To have sex with a fourteen year-old? If you can't get a girlfriend your own age? Nowadays you could be
imprisoned. Not that it happens ever.
These are the kids that the girls wouldn't look twice at in school, but when they grow older they hang around the school gates and just because of their age, and because they have cars they

but at the time

at the time I believed I was deeply in love.

Physically
I mean our bodies aren't fully formed by then are they? And our minds. Who I was at fourteen
I changed so much even from month to month. To make a decision as big as that

I could have a thirty-six year-old child, daughter, son. Thirty-six.

How can a fourteen year-old commit to having a thirty-six year-old child?
If you see what I mean.

I consented. I remember it being my decision, but

for most people I know, losing their virginity
was
well, it was a
non-event. The women anyway. They wanted
it gone.

I was sure that my mother would know. That
she'd see it in my face. In my voice, she'd hear it.

Of course she never did.

Perhaps it's just something that happens
though. Something we've just got to live with. A rite of
passage. With the number of atrocities that happen every
day it's extremely petty, isn't it, to worry about something
that's

I mean some of the things that you've all been
through.

Here's me.
I've got no right really.

It's not as if sex kills you I suppose. If almost
every grown-up survived the experience, why worry about
it? We're never going to have to go through it again.

We'll never be children again.

Listen to me. I'm
I don't know what I'm talking about someone
please

how dare I talk about this in front of

I wasn't forced. I was never forced. It was my
decision. Mine.
But

what am I saying?

I just want my daughter to lead a long, happy,
safe life.

I just
I just

perhaps I should get a hobby.

LORETTA sits down.

Some of the other GROUP MEMBERS applaud limply.

She stands back up again.

Sorry. Sorry.

I
I started to look for him.
I typed his name into the internet but

then I went to the library. I wasn't quite sure
what I was looking for.

Eventually, and I know it sounds obvious now, but I looked in the phonebook. There he was.

I'm going to meet him.

I know it's a bad idea.

Sophie and I are going up next week. Stay in a hotel. Visit my mother. And at some point I'm going to meet him.

I wondered, the other day, I was thinking, what if it was my first love? What if the tacky pop songs and Hallmark cards are right? What if when I see him I suddenly get struck down by the overwhelming feeling of first love I've suppressed these past three and a half decades?

Or

what if everything suddenly becomes clear and I remember the event for what it was, the grooming of a naïve girl? What if I'm

I don't know what I'm expecting. I want something to happen though. Something where I can say, right, that's the situation. He's a good guy. It was a genuine thing and he'd never hurt a fly. Or that he's clearly a bad guy. Or, you know.

I want to know. I want to know one way or the other.

This case, this murder that's happened

I can't help feeling that I'm responsible.

That's crazy isn't it? I mean, that's self-aggrandisement or delusion or whatever.

But whenever I see it on the news or in the paper

I just feel utterly ashamed and guilty.

After a long while, LORETTA sits back down again. She looks at her glass.

Oh look. The ice has melted.

4

Hotel bathroom. Sink, mirror, white towels hanging on silver bars. The floor and walls are covered in white tiles. A white bathrobe hangs on the back of the door. The bath is almost full and steaming, the taps running.

SOPHIE is brushing her teeth. LORETTA sits on the side of the bath, running her hand around in the water. She is contemplative.

There is a long silence.

LORETTA Yes.

It was good to see her anyway even if she is a bit

it's sad though isn't it? Just sits there.

Well.

This isn't so bad is it? You and me. Not much of a hotel.

Alright though.

Strange to be back here. Particularly with all the news. Horrible isn't it?

LORETTA turns the taps off.

Poor girl.

They think it's the same guy. You know, who they arrested for the other one?

I think they just hope it is.

40

I've got to go somewhere tomorrow. Just for a little while.

Okay?

SOPHIE spits.

Won't be gone long.

You might want to run a little more hot in.
I'll leave the door open okay? So we can talk.

LORETTA stands and leaves the room, half closing the door. SOPHIE goes to the door and pushes it a little more shut. She turns off the light, leaving only the duller shaving light above the mirror, then stands very still for a while.

She turns to the sink. She takes her jacket off and puts it over the mirror.

She starts the taps running again, quite slowly and quietly.

She opens a toiletries travel bag and takes out a pair of nail scissors.

She gets into the bath fully clothed and sits with her knees bunched up to her chest.

She opens the scissors and grips one of the blades between her thumb and forefinger.

She pushes the blade into her left wrist and runs it down along the vein for about two inches. Blood immediately begins to stream out. She closes her eyes for a moment. With a little difficulty, she repeats the process on the other wrist.

She lies back in the water.

LORETTA   (*Offstage.*)
It was fun today wasn't it? Shopping?
We could go shopping when I get back tomorrow. How about that?

Or the cinema.

I don't know what's on.

We could play it by ear.

I'd love to take you to the cinema I always used to go to. Lovely art deco building. But it's a bingo hall now.

We could go to the bingo I suppose.

SOPHIE submerges her head, just her face breaks the water line.

Everything around here has changed so much. So many of the small shops have gone. There's a Starbucks. The streets all look the same up here as they do down by us.
So do the people.

Great Frappuccino though. Starbucks.

I'm just looking at what we bought today. I'd forgotten about the wings. You know, the angel wings. They're great aren't they?

I can't imagine when either of us will wear them. I suppose they're for hen nights and things. Dress up.

There's a big mall now. If we go back the way we came and take, remember the bypass road, or maybe the one after that that we nearly took, if we go that way we'll get to the mall. We should go there tomorrow. Go shopping.

That'll be fun won't it?

Shoes?

The bath begins to overflow.

I'm going to try my wings on.

You alright in there?

Yes, so I shouldn't be gone long tomorrow. An hour at most. Maybe less. Probably will be.

You alright in there darling?

Darling?

LORETTA appears at the door. She is wearing a small pair of white wings. She knocks quietly.

Darling is everything alright?

Sweetheart?

She waits a moment longer, then peers around the door. It takes her a moment to realise what she's seeing.

She throws the door open and turns on the light. In the glaring white of the electric light the blood-red of the water is horrifying.

LORETTA rushes across to SOPHIE and climbs into the bath. She picks up her daughter, who begins to thrash about, fitting. SOPHIE's hand leaves a long smear of blood across the white tiles.

Oh no. No. No no no no no no no no no no no no no no no.

No.

No.

No.

LORETTA pulls a towel from the rack and wraps it tightly around SOPHIE's wounds. Blood quickly starts to soak through.

SOMEBODY.
SOMBODY HELP.
HELP PLEASE SOMEBODY.

The red water continues to overflow. SOPHIE is extremely pale and limp.

No no no no no no no no stay stay stay with me.

Stay with me, come on.
La la la la la.
Come on.
Come on.
Stay with me.
SOMEBODY.

SOMEONE.

Someone's coming. It's okay. Ssshhhhhhhh.

Ssshhhhhhhh.
That's it.
That's it.
Come on.

LORETTA holds her daughter tightly, rocking her back and forth.
She holds SOPHIE's face.

Come on, look at me.
Open your eyes stay with me.

That's it.
That's it.

Stay with me now.
Look at me.
Open your eyes, that's it.

SOPHIE's eyes open a fraction.

That's it darling. That's it.
La la la la la la la.

Wake up now. It's just a dream.
Just a dream.
Stay with me.
Keep looking at me.

Ssshhhhhhhhhh.

You can't do this.
You can't
          you can't know yet what life is going to be
like. You're too young to make a decision like this.

It gets better.

I promise.

Next year you'll be a different person. Even
better.

And the year after that.

Just hang in there.
Play it safe till you're all grown up.

Don't do anything rash till
don't do anything rash.

The world isn't such a bad place.
Downstairs, for instance

downstairs, in the room directly below this
there is a

it's just a regular room. Armchairs, television,
sofa. Minibar.

Are you listening?

Come on darling.

And there's plants. The most beautiful flowers
and wonderful

and it's raining. The water from the bath is
overflowing and it's it's it's seeping through the floor and
it's falling from the ceiling.

And the room looks like it's crying. It's weeping.

The the the wallpaper,
        the wallpaper is saturated. It's all peeling away from the walls. The carpet is a foot or so deep with water. There are the most beautiful fish you've ever seen swimming around.

The lights flicker.

There are tropical birds of all different colours, perched on the bookshelves.

But it's happy. The room is crying out of happiness.

LORETTA rocks her daughter back and forth.

We don't have to move, we can stay here as long as you like.

The lights flicker again.

I should probably turn the taps off though.

There is a loud bang on the door. The lights buzz loudly before cutting out to black.

5

Outside a casualty ward. It is raining. A distant light flashes blue and red across the wall.

A heavily PREGNANT YOUNG WOMAN enters, wearing a hospital maternity gown and carrying a drip-feed connected to her arm. On her other arm hangs a pink handbag with a red heart shape on it. She has makeup smudged down her face.

> *She stops, looks up and holds her hand out.*
> *She runs wet hands over her face.*
> *She slowly finds cover in a doorway.*

LORETTA enters, holding a mobile phone in one hand and a scrap of paper in the other. She is wrapped up in a raincoat and has an umbrella.

> *She dials a number written on the paper.*
> *She holds the phone to her ear, extremely nervously.*
> *Someone on the other end picks up. She is about to speak when she panics and hangs up.*

She notices the PREGNANT WOMAN.

> *The woman catches her eye.*
> *LORETTA smiles.*

The PREGNANT WOMAN takes a cigarette from a packet in her bag, puts it in her mouth and lights it.

LORETTA watches her in absolute horror.

LORETTA's telephone starts to ring.

> *She looks at the number, considers for a long while, then answers it.*
> *She holds the phone up to her ear and listens to the person on the other end.*
> *Once again, she impulsively hangs up.*
> *She stares at the phone.*

She becomes aware of the PREGNANT WOMAN looking at her.

LORETTA turns to her and tries to speak, finding the words to explain herself.

The WOMAN takes another drag on her cigarette and LORETTA loses her train of thought.

LORETTA checks her watch.

The PREGNANT WOMAN is sniffing. She starts to cry quietly but deeply.

LORETTA ignores her for as long as possible.

Eventually, she takes a few clean tissues from her pocket and cautiously offers them to the woman.

The woman stares at the tissues for a moment, then takes them.

After a little thought, LORETTA gives the WOMAN her umbrella.

The WOMAN takes it and walks on, away from the hospital.

LORETTA stands in the rain watching her go.

Her phone starts to ring. For a moment, she doesn't react.

She takes her phone and looks at the number.

She answers it.

LORETTA   Yes?

Barnaby? Barnaby Castle?

Yes I did. I

I used to live in the area. I used to know you. It's

I'd like to meet.

6

Aquarium. LORETTA sits on a small bench, her back to us, in front of a large glass window. The tank has been drained of water, but still contains large plastic boulders and ornamental castles like an oversized goldfish bowl. LORETTA has a leather handbag over her shoulder.

She is looking at her watch.

After a moment, BARNABY appears. He is in his late fifties but looks much older.

LORETTA   Barnaby?

He sees her.

LORETTA seems suddenly very frightened and full of emotion. She stands. Her manner seems to regress to being almost that of a child.

I didn't think you'd

the time, it's just closing.

BARNABY looks around.

this tank used to have sharks in. Do you remember? They were my favourite thing. But they've emptied it. Drained it.

I've been watching someone in a red boiler suit scrubbing the walls.

It's so warm isn't it? It's like an incubator in here.

I didn't know where else to meet. We used to come here, remember? On the phone I wasn't sure if you remembered me.

She laughs, nervously. Her face quickly becomes stony once more.

Loretta. Spencer.

Your father was friends with mine.

You look so different. I can see it's you, but
how've you been? I wanted to ask, I know it must seem strange me contacting you after all this time, but I wanted to meet with you and see if
well, to see if you were still

sorry. Sorry. I'm wasting your time. I know you don't have long so I'll
there's
there's something I need to know.

She takes a deep breath.

I know this is stupid but did you know Eleanor Lucas? The little girl who
or Lucy Blake? You know what's been happening? Of course, you must. Hang on.

LORETTA opens her handbag and takes out a newspaper cutting which she hands to BARNABY.

Here. Eleanor was the first, she was the first reported missing but it was little Lucy who they found first, in that garden at the back of

She goes back into her bag, producing another cutting. BARNABY takes it and reads.

this,

then this third girl, a little older than the others, you know, I mean I know you must know about this, but I needed to know if you knew about this. I needed to see you to

I know it's stupid, really really but I just needed for you to

She goes back into her bag, pulling out more and more bits of newspaper.

just,

Tissues come out as she pulls out more and more, blister packs of paracetamol fall to the ground.

now there's another girl vanished. Gone four days. I know this is stupid. It's stupid. Isn't it?

LORETTA laughs nervously again. She is shaking.

I'm sorry. I'm sorry.

Just tell me

Articles are falling from her hands. LORETTA is breathing heavily and starting to cry.

tell me

tell me

tell me it's not you.

Tell me it's not you.

LORETTA pushes the articles into BARNABY's hands. He stares at her, bewildered.

Tell me.

Eventually she collapses onto the bench, her head in her hands.

BARNABY stays looking at her for a moment.

With much effort, BARNABY bends down and picks up everything LORETTA has dropped.

He sits down next to her and holds them out to her.

She sees him and smiles. She takes them.

I don't know what's happening to me.

The first time I came here I sat on this bench and my feet didn't touch the ground.

We used to sit here. Do you remember?

Are you married? Have you been married?
Actually, that's, sorry, that's none of my
it's irrelevant.

She begins to sort the cuttings in her hands.

She's fourteen.

LORETTA looks at BARNABY seriously.

I know that at the time, when we were

I know that I said it was
that I
I thought it was alright.

I know that it was a long time ago, but I now
know that it wasn't alright. It was very very

and I need to know whether I have, whether
I should have said something. Whether I could have
prevented

I don't know.

You don't recognise me at all.

Loretta. Little Loretta.

We

we sort of

we slept together.

Loretta.

My father used to watch you play football.

BARNABY   You're Spencer's daughter.

LORETTA   Loretta Spencer, yes. George Spencer was my

BARNABY   Spence.

Spence. Spence.
Spence.

LORETTA   Do you remember me?

He looks at her.

BARNABY You're Spencer's daughter.

LORETTA Yes.

You and I

you used to come around to the house and sometimes we'd go for a drive.

We'd come here.

You used to say that you wanted to be a musician. Or go into the army. Be a marine.

What did you end up doing?

BARNABY Musician?

LORETTA That's what you used to say.

Did you ever go into the army?

BARNABY I was never in the army.

LORETTA   The reason I wanted to meet you is that we used to go out, and

this sounds pretty ridiculous now, but, there was a big age gap.

BARNABY   How old are you?

LORETTA   How

I'm fifty.

BARNABY   I'm fifty-eight.

Not much difference.

LORETTA   No.

BARNABY   My next door neighbour's wife is eighteen years older than him.

LORETTA   That's not what I'm saying.

BARNABY   What are you saying?

LORETTA   I'm sorry if I've insulted you, I really just needed

BARNABY   what?

Listen Pet, I've got to go.

BARNABY stands.

LORETTA   Did you ever have children? I mean, do you have children?

BARNABY   He was a good man, Spence.

Dead now I suppose.

LORETTA   Yes.

BARNABY   Have I got kids? Is that what you want to know?

Have you?

LORETTA   Yes.

Daughter.

BARNABY   As I say, I've got to go.

LORETTA   Yes, of course.

BARNABY starts to walk out.

        Did you

He stops.

        did you love me?

LORETTA is trembling.

        You told me you did. I just want to know why
you said that. I haven't had many people say that to me
and I'd like to know
        I'd like to know if what happened, what we
did, if it was because you loved me. Or if it was, if

BARNABY   Lsisten love, I was young. We all make
mistakes.

LORETTA   I was fourteen.

BARNABY   So you moved down south?

LORETTA   Yes.

BARNABY Listen, I don't know what you want. Perhaps you should talk to someone, you know? Someone who'll listen.

LORETTA Yes.

BARNABY turns away once more.

You should have known better.

BARNABY stops and looks at her. He shrugs.

BARNABY leaves. LORETTA sinks back onto the bench. She gazes into the empty tank. She puts her hand against the glass.

The sound of the ocean. Gulls.

7

The seaside. Very bright sunshine.

LORETTA is sat on a pier, her legs dangling over the side. She is painting SOPHIE's fingernails. SOPHIE is eating chips from newspaper with her other hand. Long sleeves and bracelets cover her wrists. Her feet are on LORETTA's lap. They both wear black. For some time, the two just sit in silence.

LORETTA   I was surprised there were so many people.

Good send-off.
Should have seen her more really. But with everything.

SOPHIE looks out to sea.

Isn't this beautiful? Boys would wish they had fishing rods out here. They'd need some kind of competitive activity to occupy them.

She blows on the nails.

SOPHIE passes the bag of chips to her mother. She is about to take one and sees something in the newspaper.

She pulls out a fistful of chips and lets them drop into the water. The sound of gulls excitingly descending on them.

Oh no.

They've found another girl.

One they didn't know was missing.

How can they not know a little girl was missing?

LORETTA unravels the newspaper, letting all the chips fall into the sea. She becomes lost in the article for a while, before looking up at SOPHIE.

Your chips! I'm so sorry.

She sighs, screws up the paper and throws it in the sea.

Enough of that. There's nothing any of us can do about it.

LORETTA looks at SOPHIE and smiles.

Let's open them.

SOPHIE smiles. LORETTA takes out a brown envelope and offers it to SOPHIE. SOPHIE doesn't take it.
LORETTA opens it. She reads the white paper inside.

You've passed everything. A's in Chemistry and Biology. B in Physics but you can always resit. Not that a B isn't, I mean, it's fantastic. I

I'm sorry I pushed you.
Takes the pressure off though. For next year.
You could do a couple extra. Politics. I don't know if they do that. They should.

Make the world a better place.

Your decision.

LORETTA passes the paper to SOPHIE who is licking her chip fingers.

Mum would have been really proud of you.

SOPHIE looks away from her mother's beaming pride in embarrassment. LORETTA keeps gazing at her daughter, more thoughtfully.

I'm proud of you.

They look out to the sea.

SOPHIE swings her legs down and steps into the sea. She paddles. She blows on her nails.

I don't think of myself as being old. Not old. I'm not. But I don't feel middle-aged. Most of the time I still feel about fourteen.

When I was fourteen I
I had my first boyfriend.

SOPHIE looks at her.

He was older than me. I thought he was amazing.

We slept together.

Last time I was here I met up with him.
He looked so old. He didn't really remember who I was.

I know how it feels to just need to speak to somebody. I'm sorry you haven't felt you could talk to me. I haven't been listening. Being fourteen can be

SOPHIE   Mum.

LORETTA   I know.
             I should stop talking.

Fancy an ice cream?

SOPHIE smiles.

Come on then.

LORETTA stands. SOPHIE steps back up onto the pier. She puts her flip-flops on. LORETTA helps her to her feet. They hold hands and walk out of sight.

The sound of waves.

After a while the lights fade.

Printed in the USA
CPSIA information can be obtained
at www.ICGtesting.com
LVHW021002171024
794056LV00004B/1283